The Wild Parrots of Marigny

ALSO BY DIANE ELAYNE DEES

Coronary Truth

The Last Time I Saw You

THE WILD PARROTS OF MARIGNY

OF MARIGNY

Diane Elayne Dees

Querencia Press, LLC
Chicago, Illinois

QUERENCIA PRESS

© Copyright 2022
Diane Elayne Dees

All Rights Reserved

LIBRARY OF CONGRESS CATALOGING-IN-PUBLICATION DATA

ISBN 978 1 959118 05 3

www.querenciapress.com

First Published in 2022

Querencia Press, LLC
Chicago IL

Printed & Bound in the United States of America

CONTENTS

For Alison

Levee Lights

We sat on the levee for birthdays,
New Year's Eve—a bottle of champagne,
a box of sparklers, a blue-black night
lit by a cloud-veiled moon. But oh,
the lights!—twinkling from steel towers,
like white Christmas bulbs on garden obelisks,
the sparklers answering back in crisp staccato,
the moonlit wine bubbling in harmony.
That was before the crack dealers came,
before the gunfire, before the hurricane.
Now, with no one there to celebrate,
the dark grass is bare at night,
while the New Orleans moon shines on
the muddied batture, where my memories
lie, washed up and abandoned.

How to Eat a Creole Tomato Sandwich

It takes elaborate preparation.
First, you must go to Louisiana,
but not just anywhere in Louisiana—
somewhere in or near a river
parish. Only tomatoes grown
in river soil become culinary miracles.
Next, you must stand in the store,
or at the roadside stand, and soak
in the fragrance of the fruit. The bigger,
the better—a slice of a giant Creole
tomato covers a piece of bread.
Once you are heady from the perfume,
it's time to admire the oversized corona.
Pay for them, take them home,
and prepare for the hard part—the wait.
When your tomatoes are gently soft
and audaciously red, take out the knife.
Cut one slice, then behold the jewel-like
structure, moist and inviting, in shades
of scarlet and orange. You may have to sit
down, should swooning be imminent.
Do not take out your best whole grain bread;
it is not needed. Slather some mayonnaise
on your white bread of choice, add some
pepper—a bit of salt if you wish—and place
the fruit between two slices of bread.
Once you have eaten this meal, there will
be an extra step the next time you prepare it:
You will stare at the sandwich in awe,
you may even feel tears forming, and you will
prepare yourself for the sadness that is to come
when you have devoured the last crumb.

Acidic Truth

The problem with the last Creole tomato
sandwich of the season is that you never
know that you've just eaten it. Even as July
comes to an end, you convince yourself
that there's still a basket at a roadside stand,
or a leftover bin at the grocery store.
And so you continue to reverently devour
them, but perhaps not reverently enough,
and one day—you discover that they are gone.
You have eaten them all, and now
you have to wait almost a year for the next
appearance of what must be the tomatoes
they eat in heaven—the huge, red near-globes
whose slices appear geologic in their juicy
complexity. You know the pleasure has to end,
but your wishful thinking—like a light sprinkling
of salt and a sharp grind of pepper—
brings out the essence of your desire, and you forget,
for a moment, that the seasons always change.

The Wisdom of Owls

The owls fled after Katrina,
but returned years later.
I hear them call
in the depths of night,
a plaintive cry
for all the lost wisdom,
blown away like
the uprooted pines.

Before the Hurricane

the chill
as tall trees sway
in unhurried warning

the smell
of stormy flint
as the sky turns green

the silence
when the birds and frogs
have fled to hidden places

the urgency
to prepare one cup of tea
before everything goes dark

When the Chainsaws Stopped

When the chainsaws stopped buzzing,
I heard green cardinals calling
red mates to sunset dinner.
When the chainsaws stopped whirring,
I heard squirrels scrambling up pine trees
in search of their homes, long blown
across blurs of highway.
When the chainsaws stopped whining,
I heard the news on the radio—
that we do not know how to help
ourselves; we are the new welfare queens,
drowning in a lake of self-pity,
our American know-how lost somewhere
between the Superdome
and the middle of next week.
When the chainsaws stopped humming,
I heard the levee crack, then the silence
of the lost, broken only
by the occasional crunch
of car wheels on debris.

Things to Do While You Wait for the Roofer

Try to find your friends.
They are probably tied up in traffic
somewhere in Texas and will be back
soon, except for those who will
never get off the highway.
You remember the last time you stood
in their houses; you picture the antique tables,
the blue Scandinavian dishes, the rose-colored depression
glasses, the shelves of books and photographs.
They are all waterlogged, smashed, reeking of mold,
or gracing the halls of looters. Your friends do not want
to talk to you, anyway. They have talked enough
to adjusters, landlords, tenants, attorneys, bureaucrats.

Find a stump grinder. Hire a brick mason. Do something
about the ripped-off gutter. Put the mailbox on a log
so the cable company can knock it off again.
Leave home an hour early because the traffic is so bad.
Throw the dead plants away. Wonder where the owl went.
Adjust to the bare patches in your yard. Wait weeks for packages
to arrive. Feel guilty because you lost some trees and some time
and your roof is wrecked, but your friends are in Texas,
and people you do not know are in trailers
if they are really, really lucky.
Feel guilty because you complain while others have no jobs
or cannot find their beloved dogs and cats or their dead mothers.

Drive to New Orleans and marvel at how easily
you can find a parking place now. Momentarily forget yourself
and try to visit your old haunts. Count the refrigerators
on each block. Go to Lakeview and see the empty houses,
the cars left in parking lots, tossed together—giant playing pieces
on a board game. Banks, restaurants, coffee shops, schools,
churches, gas stations, grocery stores, pharmacies, gift shops
all dark, abandoned, boarded. A couple in gas masks inspect
a house. The park is brown brush, the roses and red trains gone,
the carousel horses all dressed up with no place to go.
Keep your mouth closed if you can.

Pour yourself a drink and watch the news.
Get a grip on your rage.

Life Goes On

Months after the funeral, when the casserole dishes
are stacked like the vaults in St. Louis Cemeteries,
and the letters and cards have stopped coming—
that is when everyone says, "What a shame,
so youthful, so full of life, so sudden, so tragic."
"I went there once on business."
"I liked to go for Mardi Gras."
The survivors wander down empty streets,
looking for artifacts of the imperfect, but treasured,
past: a song, a taste, an anecdote—anything
that connects them to the beloved. The death
is called a suicide by some, a murder by others,
but is officially recorded as an accident,
and accidents do happen, and life is for the living.
But the forgotten survivors do not count; too much
is required to meet their needs, and anyway, grieving
is a private matter. Time heals all wounds.
Let the dead bury the dead.
Laissez le bons temps rouler.

A Decade Blown By

Huddled under an unconscious haze
of faded blue roof, we still begin
sentences with "Before Katrina"
and "After Katrina." Never quite sure
whether something—a shop, a clinic,
a way of life—still exists, we search
the Internet, do the mental inventory,
consult each other. We talk in code:
"He's aged," "It's gone,"
"...when the trees were there."
Some started over, some went away
and never came back. Some died,
some drift silently by in a rolling
fog of Xanax and uninvited memories.
Katrina weeds choke the perennials
in our yards—daily reminders
that none of our landscapes
will ever be the same.

Katrina Anniversary Song

corrupt Corps, Federal flood
blue roofs, insurance scams
trashed car, no house
no phone, no job
abandoned pets, missing corpses
toxic water, staph infections
black mold, asthma worse
dying patients, floating caskets
gangs of looters, schools gone
Danziger Bridge, shot in the back
lead exposure, can't think
murdered dogs, suicide
recurring nightmares, lifetime Xanax
blame the victims, heck of a job

Where the Pines Went

First, the bankers came, followed closely
by people with fax machines, ice cream
cones, cellular phones, polo shirts, margaritas,
floral bouquets, bagels, and bins of rubber ducks.
They brought down the pines, leaving birds
and squirrels without nests, rabbits and raccoons
without homes, and forcing deer into hoods
of SUVs. Gone are the foxes, gone the meadows,
gone the smell of pine resin when the breezes
swirl slowly from the river.

Next came Katrina. The pines swayed
precariously, their needles turned inside out
like useless umbrellas in blinding rain.
The tall trees fell, crushing gutters, breaking
windows, smashing roofs. The tree people
came and took them away, leaving only the oak
and birch for burning. The tree people stared
at the sky and saw threatening silhouettes,
and more pines fell. Those with pines still standing,
used sharpened fear to mow down survivors.
The sound of chainsaws became so normal,
we heard it even in our sleep.

The pine bark beetles were next. Too many
rotting trunks, too little help from those in charge—
the bugs, their appetites stoked to the point of no return,
marched stealthily in great armies, with no regard
for insurance, damage claims, FEMA inspections,
or anyone's proclaimed innocence. They ate their way
through residential and commercial, garden and farm,
modest property and gated community. So, the tree people
returned, and took down hundreds more; now,
outside my windows, I see a moonscape of unground stumps
where a verdant canvas once defined my space.

Who will come next to cut down the sheltering pines
that murmured to Evangeline, the cherished trees
of my childhood? Outside my window, a few still sway
silently in an early spring breeze, waiting to drop
their burden of cones, gifts we took for granted
before we heard the grinding of the saws.

Porch Gardens of New Orleans

Scattered along uptown streets
like freeform gemstones on strips
of worn green velvet, tiny yards flash
summer color across a hazy screen.
Zinnias of carnelian and garnet,
and spires of salvia with sapphire flames
singe petals of daylilies, which close
like citrine-studded lockets,
protecting their treasures from those
who stand too close to the family jewels.
Antique roses cascade iron fences
like pink abalone pearls draped
over heirloom bedposts.
Above the color-drenched display,
banana trees glimmer with tiny diamonds
of rainwater. Quicksilver clouds pry open
a window in the sky, making room
for the resplendent oaks and palmettos
that guard the city's best-kept secrets.

Shrove Tuesday, Northshore

It's Mardi Gras, and the streets are empty.
In late afternoon, the moon rolls slowly
in the sky, floating under rippled clouds—
emerging as a silver sphere, a dove gray globe,
then a ghostly, glowing white ball.
This rhythmic rotation continues
as the only Carnival show in town,
but it is enough. Walking among the pines,
I see no brightly festooned floats,
no fake gold and silver coins
or plastic beads flying through the air.
The display in the sky is more subtle,
but it stops me in my tracks.
Meanwhile, there is a parade of personal failures,
global crises, and the ghosts of all those
lives lost to a pandemic allowed to roll
through cities and towns on the wheels
of ignorance, denial and delusion.
I continue to walk, wondering if,
behind the rolling moon,
there is any hope for absolution.

Progress Report

Tar balls appear thirty miles from my front door.
In the early morning and near dusk, the perfume
of pines—even the familiar rot of Louisiana summer—
are vanquished by the smell of oil. After so many
dispersant-soaked red eye mornings, after so many
cracked pelican eggs and broken promises,
after so many withheld respirators, crushed baby
birds, unsent paychecks, and daily reports
of shortcuts, flimflams, and hands passing cash—
as the coastline disappears
and people still begin conversations
with "Before Katrina..."—what we have
to show are tar balls. Rolling in the Rigolets
Pass, dangerously near Lake Pontchartrain,
souvenirs of the spill, detritus of lost hope,
thirty miles from my front door.

Sounds

Crack of brown pelican eggs,
smash of chicks under oily boots,
crush of tern nests beneath giant tires—
sounds of BP cleanup

Splash of Corexit into the Gulf,
whoosh of oil spouting from dolphins,
rustle of marsh grass as dying birds flee—
sounds of BP cleanup

Curses of workers still waiting for pay,
gasps of crew members with no respirators,
unheard cries of widows and children—
sounds of BP cleanup.

The Great Hayward and Obama Spills
(found poetry)

What the hell did we do to deserve this?
The Gulf of Mexico is a very big ocean;
the environmental impact of this disaster
is likely to be very, very modest.
I don't think my job is on the line;
we're sorry for the massive disruption it's caused.
I would like my life back.

...I made a hurtful and thoughtless comment.
Where legitimate claims are made,
we will be good for them.

I have not spoken to him directly;
when you talk to a guy like a BP CEO,
he's going to say all the right things to me.
I would love to vent,
I would love to just shout and holler,
...I'm thinking about this day in and day out,
But my main job is to solve the problem.

Wearing Thin
"Endless Contract Negotiations Wearing Thin on Drew Brees"
Front page headline, *New Orleans Times-Picayune*

Endless crime wears thin on residents and tourists.
The man shot dead while holding his baby outside
the Bayou Boogaloo was only twenty-one;
he fell in front of his mother, who will soon enough
be worn from grief and trauma. The paint
on abandoned Ninth Ward houses has worn very thin,
the neighborhood dredged to within an inch
of its life, its foundation unable to absorb
the overflow of rivers of abandonment.
The Saints are hardly martyrs, but are made so
by masses of starving believers. They wait,
with eyes toward heaven,
while Drew Brees is worn thin.

Live Music

The jazz band plays "Bye Bye Blues"
to end the final set of the evening,
and I am transported to a time, decades ago,
when flood waters poured through
New Orleans, shutting down businesses,
destroying rugs, raising an ancient fear
among residents. The next morning,
three of us walked through an abandoned
French Quarter, where rain-blessed
banana leaves glowed like bright green
fan blades. With no cars, no tourists, no music,
no horse hooves, all we could hear
was the sloshing of our shoes—until we heard
the plaintive strains of "Bye Bye Blues"—
a woman's voice carried through
the mineral-charged, still air at the edge
of Jackson Square. She wore a long skirt
and sang through a megaphone
to an audience of three. The clarity
of her voice shook my body; the sevenths
shot up my spine. Now, sitting in a folding chair
outside a rustic old jazz hall, I am overcome
by the ozone perfume of my youth, and I sigh
deeply. In my mind's ear, eternal notes pushed
through a megaphone still radiate, and—
in spite of myself—I do not cry.

In Praise of Snowy Egrets

Like floating origami, they glide by,
their pleated wings the very essence
of aviation; surely the sight of them
inspired the first kite. On the dullest day,
they are whitest white against stippled sky,
lines and angles juxtaposed on bark and brick,
standing gracefully even in algae-clouded
ditches. Their wings flap over my garden
in DaVinci-inspired grace; they startle me
on the side of the highway, where they feed,
bent like ballet dancers in tableau.
Soft crest, needle beak, crane legs—
the daily poem of my habitat.

Egret Trinity

A pale, graceful sculpture,
the elegant bird—its legs angled
like a Bauhaus base—
stands perfectly still
before stepping into the water.
Beneath, the egret's shadow
forms a curious ink drawing
on the grass, while just beyond,
in the algae-painted pond,
the bird's reflection—a ghostly
Rorschach—ripples a message
I cannot decipher. Three egrets
stand, recline and float
before me, and I, a witness
to sacred art, am rendered
as still as the water at my feet.

At Lake Martin

In April at Lake Martin,
snowy egrets nest in cypress
like fragments of clouds dropped
from Louisiana sky, an afterthought
of heaven. Egret mothers by the hundreds
gather thousands of strands of nesting fabric.
They glide white over water
to neighboring woods, then back,
their straw baskets of vines and twigs
drooping from elegant heads.

Tufts of Spanish moss are swamp scarves
draped on tupelo: *Nyssa aquatica,*
the water nymph who shrouded the river
when Evangeline made her mournful trip
down the Atchafalaya, never again
to lay eyes on *Acadie.*

When the evening sky turns pink,
it is hard to tell the logs from the alligators.
All is not hushed; there is a mesmerizing rhythm
in the orchestra of owls, frogs and insects
who sweep the dream path clear for nestlings.

The night is sapphire, but for the golden orbs
of owls who watch the moon and listen to the pines
murmur their secrets. They wait for morning,
and the new pink sky. Soon there will be fresh pink
in the cypress limbs. Roseate spoonbills mass
the trees just down the path from the white forest
of egrets. Pink mothers perch high,
a dream of strawberry ice,

complete with spoons, waiting
to feed the rosiest-cheeked babies.

Mist covers Lake Martin,
blurring the white and pink,
floating through miles of ancient branches,
laying a soft veil over the swamp,
hiding it from the world.

Spilled Watercolors

"The Mississippi River delta looking like somebody spilled their watercolors" astronaut/photographer Jessica Meir

From space, the aqua, cream, azure, and cerulean
appear as if blended by a master painter
with an eye for serenity and expansion. I imagine
a second painting, this one bright, yet soft,
with puffs of spoonbill pink and splashes
of sea turtle green streaked across a peaceful
background of bunting indigo. From space,
the Louisiana delta is an impressionist's dream
of water and feathers and the reflections
of a marbled sky. Up close, the picture tears
at the edges as the coastline rapidly recedes.
The Rusty Blackbird, black bear and Great Blue
fade behind a foreground of erosion and loss.
From space, the watercolors spill a dream-like
beauty onto a canvas teeming with life,
while the landscape shifts precariously,
altering the perspective forever.

Louisiana Blue

The Manchac's banks are blessed with indigo
when native iris saturate the view
in April. When the moss is hanging low,
the cypress and the mighty tupelo
give shelter to the Great and Little Blue.
A dash of azure caps the vireo;
the deepest cobalt ink seems to imbue
the bunting, with its iridescent glow.
A bright blue lizard shuttles to and fro.
As purple twilight heralds its debut
and merges softly with the bayou's flow,
the stippled sky takes on a darker hue,
lending the swamp its gentle afterglow.
The Manchac's banks are blessed with indigo;
Louisiana sleeps in folds of blue.

Lament For Louisiana

Each day the fragile coastline slips away,
a sedge, a heron's home, an eagle's nest,
will vanish before the sky folds into gray.

The egrets in the Atchafalaya Bay,
the marsh hen with its shining azure crest—
each day the fragile coastline slips away,

leaving no safe place for them to stay.
The spoonbill with the banded golden breast
will vanish. Before the sky folds into gray,

you still can see a glorious display,
as the roseate sun glides slowly to the west
each day. The fragile coastline slips away

as bold raccoons and river otters play.
The black bear, who was once a welcome guest,
will vanish before the sky folds into gray.

The rich blue view of iris in array
alongside swamp rose mallow finely dressed—
each day the fragile coastline slips away—
will vanish before the sky folds into gray.

Storm Debris

We have seen it before:
the downed trees, the piles of limbs,
shingles flung to the street,
dozens of overflowing trash cans
reeking of rotted vegetables.
We know the drill—
the power will come back on
some day. There will be cable TV
and Internet someday,
and when we least expect it,
our phones will work again.

We are tough, we are resilient,
but we are powerless to escape
the sounds—the roar of generators,
the constant buzz of saws—the sounds
of Katrina. They blow through
the deepest recesses of our psyches,
they flow like restless bayous
through our waking dreams.

We knew then that we would never
be the same. Our hair stopped growing,
or it fell out or turned suddenly gray.
The displaced, with their glazed-over eyes,
were easy to recognize. The rest of us
shuddered every time we saw the images.
Our bodies tightened like vises
every time the talking heads told a story
that had *nothing* to do with what happened.

We hear the droning symphony of saws
and motors—the sounds that remind us
that our DNA has been altered,
and that future generations will bear these genes.
The never-ending soundtrack of Katrina
is background music for the movie
that will never stop running—people
crammed onto the floor of the Superdome,
beloved pets tossed into the street to drown,
the sound of bullets on the Danziger Bridge,
deputies entering houses and shooting dogs,
the caskets of long-dead relatives
floating down the street, the deadly effects
of black mold and lead poisoning,
the remains of looted stores,
the search for missing corpses,
the leader eating cake in the desert.

Suddenly, there are birds
and dragonflies again,
and one morning, the sun shines.
At some point, generators will shut down,
and the saws will be put away.
But their sounds remain,
vibrating through our cells,
a deadly signature unique to us—
the eternal hum of trauma.

The Wild Parrots of Marigny

On a Marigny balcony at dusk,
amid tangles of philodendron and vines
creeping from cracked, weathered pots,
I allow the city to seep into my skin.
Breathing deeply, I inhale thick
familiar air—molecules swirling with fog
and jasmine, spilled beer and spices,
damp earth and the gentle perfume
of porch gardens. The parrots fly
above my head, stopping to sample
fruit from a nearby mayhaw. People say
the birds were in New Orleans long ago,
but disappeared, along with landmarks
still mourned by natives.
Katrina brought them back, one more mystery
of the storm, blown in like the seeds
whose giant flowers startle passersby.
They glide toward my head,
graceful actors in a seduction
against which I have little defense.

As they fly away, I descend to the street,
where the still-handsome old artist—
the one who left his mark on Mapplethorpe—
rides his bicycle amid the traffic of friends
and tourists. The years blur inside my head
like the pastels and shadows of his drawings.
The sight of him pedaling past tiny jungles
and ancient buildings startles me,
and I remember the parrots.
The emerald messengers returned
when they were most needed,

when survivors—starved for hope,
thirsting for beauty—needed a sign.
"Come back," the parrots say; I hear them
on every street, and all the way up
the wobbly stairs to the little Italian restaurant.

Later, drunk on the city, I sleep the fitful sleep
of one who, emboldened by time, dares
to taste a forbidden substance. I leave
the next day, but the wild parrots of Marigny
continue to fly through my dreams, circling my head,
brushing against endless memories,
chattering the sacred rhythm of the city,
disturbing my peace.

Waiting Out the Storm on Magazine Street

The flaming orange of the snowball,
the sharp-sweet taste of mango,
the purple house across the street,
the man in the turquoise chair slipping
me a wink while his wife tells a story,
the chair I bought on impulse,
waiting for me in the blue car
now luminous with New Orleans rain,
rushing down suddenly,
washing me transparent with joy.

Notes on Previous Publication

Main Channel Voices: "Levee Lights"
Prometheus Dreaming: "How to Eat a Creole Tomato Sandwich"
Willawaw Journal: "Acidic Truth"
ONE ART: "The Wisdom of Owls"
Autumn Sky Poetry Daily: "Before the Hurricane"
Hurricane Blues: Poems about Katrina and Rita: "Things to Do While You Wait for the Roofer"
Jerry Jazz Musician: "Live Music"
Muscadine Lines: "Life Goes On," "In Praise of Snowy Egrets"
SubtleTea: "A Decade Blown By"
The New Verse News: "Katrina Anniversary Song," "Spilled Watercolors"
Spillway Review: "Porch Gardens of New Orleans," "At Lake Martin"
Delta Poetry Review: "Shrove Tuesday, Northshore"
Poets for Living Waters: "Progress Report"
protest poems: "Sounds"
Poetry Super Highway: "The Great Hayward and Obama Spills"
Poetry Breakfast: "Wearing Thin"
Amethyst Review: "Egret Trinity"
The Eleventh Muse: "Louisiana Blue"
The Raintown Review: "Lament for Louisiana"
Sparks of Calliope: "Storm Debris"
Lucid Rhythms: "The Wild Parrots of Marigny"
Peacock Journal: "Waiting Out the Storm on Magazine Street"

www.ingramcontent.com/pod-product-compliance
Lightning Source LLC
Chambersburg PA
CBHW061328120626
46546CB00007B/2717